500

QUIZ

ON

TAYLOR
SWIFT

SANJU SHARMA

This
book
belongs
to

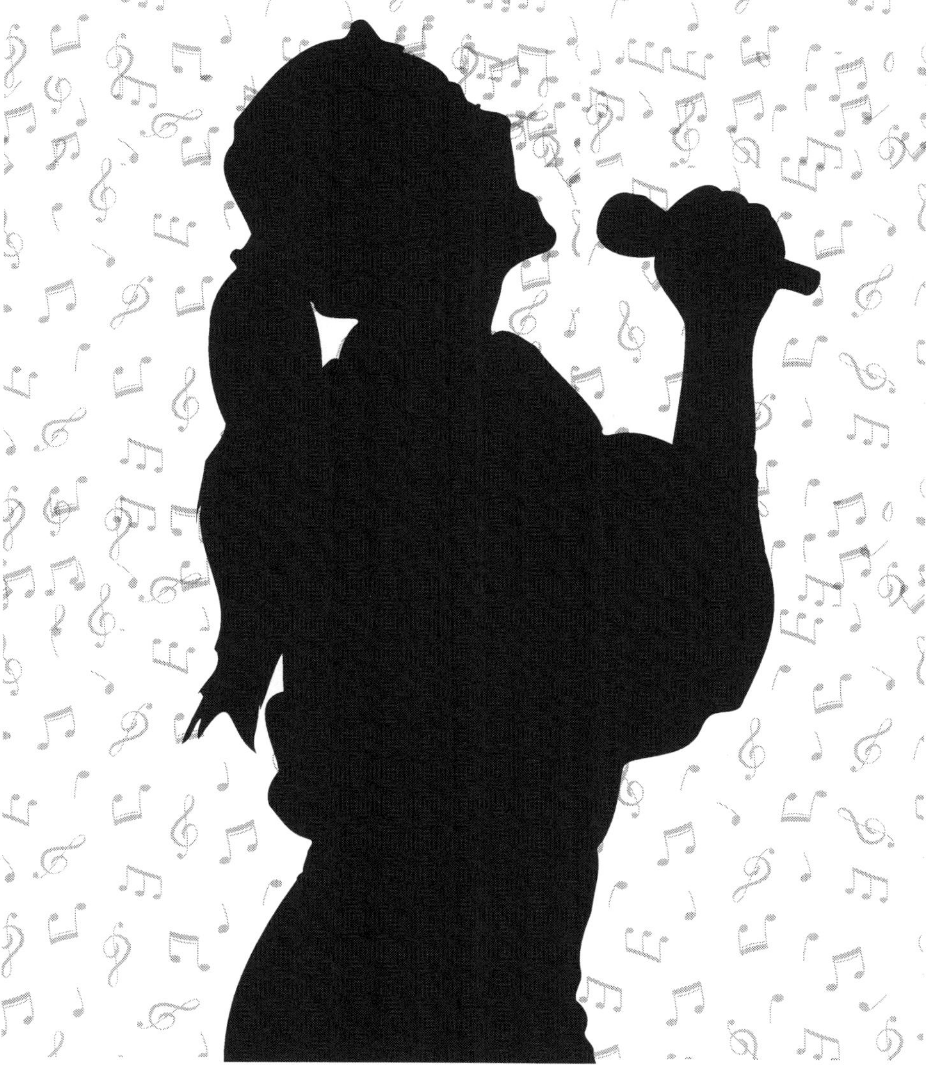

CONTENTS

1. What is Taylor Swift's birth date?

A) November 13, 1988
B) December 13, 1989
C) January 13, 1990
D) February 13, 1991

2. What is Taylor Swift's full name?

A) Taylor Gardner Swift
B) Taylor Alison Swift
C) Taylor Finlay Swift
D) Taylor Andrea Swift

3. Taylor Swift was born in which city?

A) Nashville, TN
B) Pennsylvania's West Reading
C) New York, New York City
D) California's Los Angeles

4. What is the name of Taylor Swift's brother?

A) Austin Swift
B) Ethan Swift
C) Dylan Swift
D) Mason Swift

5. What was Taylor Swift's father's profession?

A) Stockbroker
B) Musician
C) Doctor
D) Lawyer

6. Taylor Swift's mother previously worked as a?

A) Chef
B) Homemaker
C) Marketing Executive
D) Teacher

7. In which town did Taylor Swift attend high school?

A) Nashville
B) Wyomissing
C) Hendersonville
D) Stone Harbor

8. At what age did Taylor Swift become interested in musical theater?

A) 9
B) 11
C) 14
D) 12

9. Which artist inspired Taylor Swift to shift her focus to country music?

A) Shania Twain
B) Faith Hill
C) Dolly Parton
D) Dixie Chicks

10. Who taught Taylor Swift to play the guitar?

A) Shania Twain
B) Ronnie Cremer
C) Dan Dymtrow
D) Faith Hill

11. At what age did Taylor Swift travel to Nashville to pursue a music career?

A) 11
B) 13
C) 14
D) 15

12. What was the first song Taylor Swift wrote with the help of Ronnie Cremer?

A) Lucky You
B) Love Story
C) Enchanted
D) Teardrops on My Guitar

13. Which talent manager did Taylor Swift and her parents work with in New York?

A) Ronnie Cremer
B) Dan Dymtrow
C) Scott Kingsley Swift
D) Andrea Gardner Swift

14. For which brand did Taylor Swift model as part of their "Rising Stars" campaign?

A) Maybelline
B) Abercrombie & Fitch
C) Calvin Klein
D) Chanel

15. At what age did Taylor Swift sign an artist development deal with RCA Records?

A) 13
B) 14
C) 15
D) 16

16. Which high school did Taylor Swift attend in Hendersonville?

A) Wyomissing Area Junior/Senior High School
B) Alvernia Montessori School
C) Hendersonville High School
D) Aaron Academy

17. At what age did Taylor Swift start performing at local festivals and events?

A) 10
B) 12
C) 14
D) 16

18. Which artist's documentary inspired Taylor Swift to pursue a career in music?

A) Shania Twain
B) Faith Hill
C) Dixie Chicks
D) Marjorie Finlay

19. In which city did Taylor Swift take vocal and acting lessons?

A) Los Angeles
B) Nashville
C) New York City
D) Chicago

20. What was the name of the Christmas tree farm Taylor Swift spent her early years on?

A) Swift Family Farm
B) Kingsley Farm
C) Gardner Tree Farm
D) Wyomissing Tree Farm

21. What was the name of the opera singer who was Taylor Swift's maternal grandmother?

A) Shania Twain
B) Faith Hill
C) Marjorie Finlay
D) Dixie Chicks

22. Which school did Taylor Swift attend for preschool and kindergarten?

A) Wyomissing Area Junior/Senior High School
B) Alvernia Montessori School
C) Hendersonville High School
D) Aaron Academy

23. Which city did Taylor Swift visit with her mother at age eleven to submit demo tapes?

A) New York City
B) Los Angeles
C) Nashville
D) Chicago

24. In 2018, Taylor Swift signed to which record label?

A) Big Machine Records;
B) Republic Records
C) Sony Music Entertainment
D) Columbia Records

25. Which of Taylor Swift's albums experimented with electronic elements?

A) Fearless
B) Speak Now
C) Red
D) Lover

26. Which Taylor Swift album features the songs "Shake It Off" and "Blank Space"?

A) Red
B) 1989
C) Reputation
D) Lover

27. What is the main source of income for Taylor Swift, making her the first billionaire?

A) Acting
B) Merchandise
C) Endorsements
D) Music

28. What is the title of Taylor Swift's autobiographical documentary released in 2020?

A) Miss Americana
B) Taylor's Version
C) Eras Tour
D) All Too Well: The Short Film

29. What is the name of Taylor Swift's debut album?

A) Fearless
B) Taylor Swift
C) Speak Now
D) Red

30. Who caught Taylor Swift's attention during an industry showcase at Nashville's Bluebird Cafe in 2005?

A) Scott Borchetta
B) Brad Paisley
C) Troy Verges
D) Liz Rose

31. In which year was Taylor Swift's debut album, "Taylor Swift," released?

A) 2004
B) 2005
C) 2006
D) 2007

32. Which song from Taylor Swift's debut album reached number thirteen on the U.S. Billboard Hot 100?

A) Teardrops on My Guitar
B) Our Song
C) Picture to Burn
D) Should've Said No

33. What did Taylor Swift's father purchase in Big Machine Records?

A) 10% stake
B) 5% stake
C) 3% stake
D) 15% stake

34. Who was Taylor Swift's producer for her debut album?

A) Scott Borchetta
B) Nathan Chapman
C) Troy Verges
D) Liz Rose

35. What accolade did Taylor Swift win at the Nashville Songwriters Association in 2007?

A) Album of the Year
B) Songwriter/Artist of the Year
C) Best New Artist
D) Horizon Award

36. Which of Taylor Swift's songs became the first female country music artist to write or co-write every track on a U.S. platinum-certified debut album?

A) Teardrops on My Guitar
B) Our Song
C) Picture to Burn
D) Should've Said No

37. Which of Taylor Swift's albums spent the longest stay on the U.S. Billboard 200 chart in the 2000s decade?

A) Fearless
B) Speak Now
C) Red
D) Taylor Swift

38. Which artist did Taylor Swift date in 2008?

A) Brad Paisley
B) Joe Jonas
C) Tim McGraw
D) Rascal Flatts

39. What was Taylor Swift's father's investment in Big Machine Records estimated to be?

A) $50,000
B) $100,000
C) $120,000
D) $150,000

40. What was the release date of Taylor Swift's second studio album, "Fearless"?

A) November 11, 2008
B) March 11, 2009
C) November 11, 2009
D) March 11, 2008

41. Which of Taylor Swift's songs from the "Fearless" album was the first country song to top Billboard's Pop Songs chart?

A) Love Story
B) White Horse
C) You Belong with Me
D) Fifteen

42. How much did Swift's first headlining concert tour, the Fearless Tour, gross?

A) $63 million
B) $50 million
C) $75 million
D) $100 million

43. Which award did the music video "You Belong with Me" win at the 2009 MTV Video Music Awards?

A) Best Female Video
B) Video of the Year
C) Best Country Song
D) Best Music Video

44. At the 52nd Annual Grammy Awards, which category did "White Horse" win?

A) Best Country Song
B) Album of the Year
C) Best Female Country Vocal Performance
D) Best Pop Song

45. Who interrupted Taylor Swift's acceptance speech at the 2009 MTV Video Music Awards?

A) John Mayer
B) Taylor Lautner
C) Kanye West
D) T-Pain

46. What was the name of the documentary miniseries about Taylor Swift's Fearless Tour?

A) Journey to Fearless
B) Fearless Expedition
C) Swift's Odyssey
D) Fearless Chronicles

47. Which song did Taylor Swift co-write and record with Kellie Pickler?

A) Love Story
B) Best Days of Your Life
C) Two Is Better Than One
D) Thug Story

48. In which year did Taylor Swift make her television debut in a CSI: Crime Scene Investigation episode?

A) 2008
B) 2009
C) 2010
D) 2011

49. What was the title of Taylor Swift's first number-one single on the Canadian Hot 100?

A) Love Story
B) You Belong with Me
C) Today Was a Fairytale
D) White Horse

50. At the 2009 Country Music Association Awards, what award did Taylor Swift win?

A) Female Video of the Year
B) Entertainer of the Year
C) Album of the Year
D) Artist of the Year

51. Who did Taylor Swift date while shooting her film debut Valentine's Day in October 2009?

A) John Mayer
B) Taylor Lautner
C) Keith Urban
D) T-Pain

52. In 2009, Swift contributed two songs to the soundtrack of which film?

A) Twilight
B) The Notebook
C) The Fault in Our Stars
D) Valentine's Day

53. Who did Taylor Swift perform as a supporting act for during the Escape Together World Tour in 2009?

A) John Mayer
B) Keith Urban
C) Boys Like Girls
D) T-Pain

54. At the 2009 MTV Video Music Awards, what incident became the subject of controversy and Internet memes?

A) Taylor Swift's performance
B) Kanye West interrupting Swift's acceptance speech
C) Swift winning Video of the Year
D) Swift's outfit

55. At the 2009 American Music Awards, how many awards did Taylor Swift win?

A) 3
B) 4
C) 5
D) 6

56. Who hosted and performed as the musical guest on Saturday Night Live, being the first host to write their own opening monologue?

A) Taylor Lautner
B) Kanye West
C) Taylor Swift
D) John Mayer

57. In the Hannah Montana: The Movie soundtrack, which songs did Taylor Swift write?

A) You'll Always Find Your Way Back Home and Crazier
B) Love Story and White Horse
C) Fifteen and Fearless
D) Today Was a Fairytale and Two Is Better Than One

58. Who was Taylor Swift's co-star in the film Valentine's Day?

A) John Mayer
B) Taylor Lautner
C) Keith Urban
D) Calvin Harris

59. Who did Taylor Swift co-write and record the song "Half of My Heart" with?

A) John Mayer
B) Taylor Lautner
C) Keith Urban
D) T-Pain

60. What was the lead single from Taylor Swift's third studio album, "Speak Now"?

A) Back to December
B) Mine
C) Sparks Fly
D) Mean

61. Which song from "Speak Now" won Best Country Song and Best Country Solo Performance at the 54th Annual Grammy Awards in 2012?

A) Back to December
B) Sparks Fly
C) Mean
D) Ours

62. In which year did Taylor Swift date actor Jake Gyllenhaal?

A) 2010
B) 2011
C) 2012
D) 2013

63. What was the lead single from Taylor Swift's fourth studio album, "Red"?

A) We Are Never Ever Getting Back Together
B) Begin Again
C) I Knew You Were Trouble
D) 22

64. Which song from "Red" became Taylor Swift's first number one in the U.S. and New Zealand?

A) Begin Again
B) I Knew You Were Trouble
C) 22
D) Everything Has Changed

65. Who did Taylor Swift briefly date during the Red Tour?

A) Conor Kennedy
B) Jake Gyllenhaal
C) Harry Styles
D) Tim McGraw

66. For which animated film did Taylor Swift voice the character Audrey?

A) The Lorax
B) Zootopia
C) Frozen
D) Moana

67. In which year did Taylor Swift receive the Pinnacle Award during the Red Tour?

A) 2012
B) 2013
C) 2014
D) 2015

68. Which Taylor Swift album did she write alone and co-produce every track?

A) Fearless
B) Speak Now
C) Red
D) 1989

69. What was the fastest-selling digital album by a female artist at the time?

A) Speak Now
B) Red
C) Fearless
D) 1989

70. At the 54th Annual Grammy Awards, which song earned Taylor Swift Best Country Song and Best Country Solo Performance?

A) Back to December
B) The Story of Us
C) Sparks Fly
D) Mean

71. What song did Taylor Swift record for the soundtrack of "The Hunger Games"?

A) Eyes Open
B) Safe & Sound
C) Everything Has Changed
D) The Last Time

72. In which year did Taylor Swift date Conor Kennedy?

A) 2011
B) 2012
C) 2013
D) 2014

73. Which of Taylor Swift's albums earned her four nominations at the 56th Annual Grammy Awards (2014)?

A) Speak Now
B) Fearless
C) Red
D) 1989

74. Which Taylor Swift song won the Grammy Award for Best Song Written for Visual Media?

A) Safe & Sound
B) Sweeter than Fiction
C) Eyes Open
D) The Last Time

75. Who did Taylor Swift provide guest vocals for on the song "Highway Don't Care"?

A) Tim McGraw
B) Keith Urban
C) Blake Shelton
D) Luke Bryan

76. In which film did Taylor Swift have a supporting role in 2014?

A) The Giver
B) The Hunger Games
C) The Lorax
D) Cats

77. At the 71st Golden Globe Awards, which song received a nomination for Best Original Song?

A) Eyes Open
B) Safe & Sound
C) Sweeter than Fiction
D) Everything Has Changed

78. What award did Taylor Swift receive during the Red Tour, making her the second recipient after Garth Brooks?

A) Grammy Award
B) Pinnacle Award
C) Artist of the Year
D) Country Music Association Award

79. What did Rolling Stone name "Speak Now" among in 2012?

A) Best Female Albums of All Time
B) Best Country Albums of All Time
C) Best Rock Albums of All Time
D) Best Pop Albums of All Time

80. In which sitcom did Taylor Swift make a cameo in 2013?

A) Friends
B) How I Met Your Mother
C) New Girl
D) The Big Bang Theory

81. What was Taylor Swift's fifth studio album released in 2014?

A) Fearless
B) Speak Now
C) Red
D) 1989

82. In which city did Taylor Swift begin living in March 2014?

A) Nashville
B) Los Angeles
C) New York City
D) London

83. Who did Taylor Swift date from March 2015 to June 2016?

A) Joe Alwyn
B) Calvin Harris
C) Tom Hiddleston
D) Ed Sheeran

84. What was the highest-grossing tour of 2015?

A) Red Tour
B) Fearless Tour
C) 1989 World Tour
D) Speak Now World Tour

85. Which streaming platform did Taylor Swift remove her entire catalog from in November 2014?

A) Spotify
B) Apple Music
C) Amazon Music
D) Google Play

86. Who did Taylor Swift successfully countersue in August 2017?

A) Kanye West
B) David Mueller
C) Calvin Harris
D) Tom Hiddleston

87. Which song did Taylor Swift co-write with Scottish DJ Calvin Harris?

A) I Don't Wanna Live Forever
B) This Is What You Came For
C) End Game
D) Delicate

88. What was the lead single from Taylor Swift's sixth album, "Reputation"?

A) Look What You Made Me Do
B) Ready for It?
C) End Game
D) Delicate

89. In which year did Taylor Swift win the Brit Award for International Female Solo Artist?

A) 2014
B) 2015
C) 2016
D) 2017

90. What did Taylor Swift criticize Apple Music for in June 2015?

A) Lack of artist royalties
B) Limited song selection
C) Poor sound quality
D) Inadequate playlist options

91. Who did Taylor Swift date after her brief relationship with Tom Hiddleston?

A) Joe Alwyn
B) Calvin Harris
C) Ed Sheeran
D) Zayn Malik

92. Which song earned Taylor Swift the Song of the Year award at the 51st CMA Awards?

A) I Don't Wanna Live Forever
B) Better Man
C) Style
D) Bad Blood

93. What pseudonym did Taylor Swift use for her contribution to Calvin Harris's song "This Is What You Came For"?

A) Emma Stone
B) Nils Sjöberg
C) Olivia Wilde
D) Lily Collins

94. Which album won Album of the Year and Best Pop Vocal Album at the 58th Grammy Awards?

A) Fearless
B) Red
C) 1989
D) Reputation

95. Which albums sold one million copies in a week in the U.S., making her the first act to achieve this?

A) Fearless
B) Red
C) 1989
D) Reputation

96. Who did Taylor Swift collaborate with on the joint single "I Don't Wanna Live Forever"?

A) Ed Sheeran
B) Zayn Malik
C) Rihanna
D) Future

97. Which song from the album "Reputation" reached the top of the charts in Australia, Ireland, New Zealand, and the U.S.?

A) Delicate
B) End Game
C) Look What You Made Me Do
D) Ready for It?

98. What was the total revenue of Taylor Swift's Reputation Stadium Tour in 2018?

A) $250 million
B) $345.7 million
C) $200 million
D) $300 million

99. At which awards ceremony did Taylor Swift win four awards, including Artist of the Year and Favorite Pop/Rock Female Artist?

A) MTV Video Music Awards
B) American Music Awards
C) Grammy Awards
D) Brit Awards

100. Which Taylor Swift album incorporated heavy electropop, hip hop, R&B, and EDM sounds?

A) Fearless
B) Red
C) 1989
D) Reputation

101. In which month and year was Taylor Swift's album "Reputation" released?

A) October 2016
B) November 2017
C) September 2015
D) December 2018

102.What exhibit opened in honor of Taylor Swift at the Grammy Museum on her 25th birthday in 2014?

A) Country Music Hall of Fame exhibit
B) Rock and Roll Hall of Fame exhibit
C) Grammy Museum exhibit
D) Smithsonian exhibit

103. What was the total attendance record broken by Taylor Swift's exhibit at the Grammy Museum in Los Angeles?

A) 100,000
B) 200,000
C) 300,000
D) 400,000

104. At the 2015 Brit Awards, what category did Taylor Swift win?

A) British Album of the Year
B) British Female Solo Artist
C) International Male Solo Artist
D) International Female Solo Artist

105. Who did Taylor Swift collaborate with on the single "Babe" released in April 2018?

A) Ed Sheeran
B) Zayn Malik
C) Calvin Harris
D) Sugarland

106. Which of Taylor Swift's albums sold over 4.5 million copies worldwide as of 2018?

A) Fearless
B) 1989
C) Red
D) Reputation

107. At the 2014 American Music Awards, what award did Taylor Swift receive?

A) Album of the Year
B) Woman of the Year
C) Dick Clark Award for Excellence
D) Artist of the Year

108. What was the title of the song released as the joint single with English singer Zayn Malik for Fifty Shades Darker: Original Motion Picture Soundtrack?

A) Delicate
B) Ready for It?
C) I Don't Wanna Live Forever
D) End Game

109. What was Taylor Swift's last album under Big Machine?

A) Reputation
B) Lover
C) Folklore
D) Evermore

110. With which record label did Taylor Swift sign a new deal in November 2018?

A) Sony Music
B) Universal Music Group
C) Republic Records
D) Big Machine

111. Who was the first female artist to have a sixth consecutive album sell more than 500,000 copies in one week in the U.S.?

A) Beyoncé
B) Adele
C) Taylor Swift
D) Rihanna

112. Which song from the album "Lover" became a resurgent success in 2023 and reached number one on the Hot 100?

A) The Man
B) You Need to Calm Down
C) Lover
D) Cruel Summer

113. In the documentary Miss Americana, which film adaptation did Taylor Swift play the character Bombalurina?

A) Les Misérables
B) Cats
C) Phantom of the Opera
D) Mamma Mia!

114. Which talent manager did Taylor Swift have a public dispute with over the purchase of the masters of her back catalog?

A) Scooter Braun
B) Simon Cowell
C) Clive Davis
D) David Geffen

115. What was the lead single from Taylor Swift's seventh studio album, "Lover"?

A) Cruel Summer
B) Me!
C) The Man
D) You Need to Calm Down

116. which song from "Lover" won Best Visual Effects at the MTV Video Music Awards?

A) Me!
B) The Man
C) Cruel Summer
D) You Need to Calm Down

117. What deal did Taylor Swift sign in February 2020 after her 16-year-old contract with Sony/ATV expired?

A) Clothing Line Deal
B) Makeup Endorsement Deal
C) Global Publishing Deal with Universal Music Publishing
D) Movie Production Deal

118. During the COVID-19 pandemic, Taylor Swift released two surprise albums. What are they?

A) Reputation and 1989
B) Fearless and Speak Now
C) Folklore and Evermore
D) Red and Taylor Swift

119. Which of Taylor Swift's albums was the world's best-selling album by a solo artist in 2019?

A) Reputation
B) Lover
C) Folklore
D) Evermore

120. In the film adaptation of Andrew Lloyd Webber's musical Cats (2019), which character did Taylor Swift play?

A) Grizabella
B) Rum Tum Tugger
C) Bombalurina
D) Mr. Mistoffelees

121. What did Taylor Swift become the first artist to debut simultaneously with "Folklore" and "Evermore"?

A) A U.S. number-one album and a number-one song
B) A Grammy Award and an Oscar
C) A clothing line and a fragrance
D) A movie and a TV show

122. Which song from "Folklore" won Album of the Year at the 63rd Annual Grammy Awards?

A) Cardigan
B) Betty
C) Exile
D) Willow

123. Who co-wrote and co-produced select songs under the pseudonym William Bowery on Taylor Swift's albums "Folklore" and "Evermore"?

A) Jack Antonoff
B) Aaron Dessner
C) Joe Alwyn
D) Louis Bell

124. Which publication emphasized that "Folklore" and "Evermore" increased Taylor Swift's artistic credibility?

A) Rolling Stone
B) The Guardian
C) Billboard
D) Variety

125. What was the 2020's best-selling album in the U.S.?

A) Lover
B) Folklore
C) Evermore
D) Reputation

126. At the 2020 American Music Awards, how many awards did Taylor Swift win, including Artist of the Year?

A) One
B) Two
C) Three
D) Four

127. Which song from "Evermore" features a collaboration with HAIM and reached mainstream success?

A) Willow
B) No Body, No Crime
C) Coney Island
D) Exile

128. In 2019, which award did Taylor Swift win at the MTV Video Music Awards for a video that she directed?

A) Best Visual Effects
B) Video of the Year
C) Video for Good
D) Best Editing

129. What genre did "Folklore" and "Evermore" explore with a more muted production compared to Taylor Swift's previous upbeat pop songs?

A) Rap
B) Indie Folk and Alternative Rock
C) Country
D) EDM

130. Which song from "Lover" earned Taylor Swift the title of the first female artist to have a sixth consecutive album sell more than 500,000 copies in one week in the U.S.?

A) You Need to Calm Down
B) Cruel Summer
C) Lover
D) Me!

131. What song from "Lover" won Video of the Year and Video for Good at the 2019 MTV Video Music Awards?

A) Me!
B) The Man
C) You Need to Calm Down
D) Cruel Summer

132. Which two producers worked with Taylor Swift on writing and recording the albums "Folklore" and "Evermore"?

A) Max Martin and Joel Little
B) Jack Antonoff and Aaron Dessner
C) Louis Bell and Frank Dukes
D) Ryan Tedder and Benny Blanco

133. At the 2020 Grammy Awards, what record did Taylor Swift set by winning Album of the Year for "Folklore"?

A) First woman to win three times
B) Youngest artist to win
C) Most nominations in one year
D) Fastest-selling album in history

134. Which Taylor Swift album sold 3.2 million copies in 2019, making it the world's best-selling album by a solo artist?

A) Reputation
B) Lover
C) Folklore
D) Evermore

135. In the 2020 Sundance Film Festival, what documentary chronicled parts of Taylor Swift's life and career?

A) Miss Americana
B) Swift: Unfiltered
C) Behind the Spotlight
D) Journey of a Songstress

136. In 2020, what did Billboard name Taylor Swift in terms of earnings?

A) Highest-paid musician in the world
B) Highest-paid actress in Hollywood
C) Highest-paid author
D) Highest-paid athlete

137. What was Taylor Swift's first studio album released after signing with Universal Music Group?

A) Red
B) 1989
C) Reputation
D) Lover

138. What was the first re-recorded album released by Taylor Swift as part of the masters dispute?

A) Speak Now (Taylor's Version)
B) Fearless (Taylor's Version)
C) Red (Taylor's Version)
D) Midnights

139. Which song from the re-recorded album "Red (Taylor's Version)" became the longest song in history to top the Hot 100?

A) Lavender Haze
B) Karma
C) Anti-Hero
D) All Too Well (10 Minute Version)

140. What genre was Taylor Swift's album "Midnights" characterized by, according to Rolling Stone critics?

A) Country
B) Pop
C) Electropop
D) Rock

141. Which award did Taylor Swift's short film accompanying "All Too Well (10 Minute Version)" win?

A) Grammy Award for Best Music Video
B) MTV Video Music Award for Video of the Year
C) Golden Globe Award for Cinematic and Box Office Achievement
D) 66th Annual Grammy Award for Song of the Year

142. In 2023, which Taylor Swift album made her the woman with the most number-one albums in Billboard 200 history?

A) 1989 (Taylor's Version)
B) Speak Now (Taylor's Version)
C) Red (Taylor's Version)
D) Midnights

143. What was the lead single from Taylor Swift's album "Midnights"?

A) Karma
B) Anti-Hero
C) Lavender Haze
D) Is It Over Now?

144. Which tour by Taylor Swift became the highest-grossing tour in history?

A) Speak Now Tour
B) Fearless Tour
C) Red Tour
D) Eras Tour

145. Which platform declared Taylor Swift as the most streamed artist of 2023?

A) Spotify
B) Apple Music
C) Amazon Music
D) YouTube

146. How much did the Eras Tour concert film earn worldwide?

A) $250 million
B) $500 million
C) $1 billion
D) $2 billion

147. Which artist did Taylor Swift collaborate with on the song "Renegade"?

A) Ed Sheeran
B) Haim
C) Big Red Machine
D) The National

148. For which film's soundtrack did Taylor Swift record the song "Carolina"?

A) Where the Crawdads Sing
B) Amsterdam
C) The Joker and the Queen
D) The Alcott

149. In which film did Taylor Swift have a supporting role in 2022?

A) The Alcott
B) Where the Crawdads Sing
C) Amsterdam
D) Midnights

150. Which Taylor Swift album became the best-selling album of 2023?

A) Fearless (Taylor's Version)
B) Midnights
C) 1989 (Taylor's Version)
D) Speak Now (Taylor's Version)

151. Who did Taylor Swift begin dating in 2023?

A) Ed Sheeran
B) Travis Kelce
C) Big Red Machine
D) The National

152. What aspect of music did Taylor Swift find most appealing in her early years?

A) Instrumental composition
B) Storytelling
C) Vocal harmonies
D) Experimental soundscapes

153. Who was Taylor Swift's biggest musical influence among female country artists of the 1990s?

A) Faith Hill
B) Shania Twain
C) Dixie Chicks
D) Loretta Lynn

154. Which iconic 1990s songwriter influenced Taylor Swift with emotional and autobiographical lyrics?

A) Joni Mitchell
B) Melissa Etheridge
C) Sarah McLachlan
D) Alanis Morissette

155. In her album "1989," Taylor Swift drew inspiration from which of the following 1980s pop acts?

A) Peter Gabriel
B) Madonna
C) Phil Collins
D) Annie Lennox

156. Which vocal register did Taylor Swift use in the song "Cardigan"?

A) Falsetto
B) Mezzo-soprano
C) Tenor
D) Baritone

157. What was Taylor Swift's description of her fifth studio album, "1989"?

A) "My first country album."
B) "My first documented, official pop album."
C) "An experiment in rock music."
D) "A return to my country roots."

158. Which album marked Taylor Swift's departure from country music in 2014?

A) Reputation
B) Lover
C) Red
D) 1989

159. Which album features Taylor Swift's experimental and subdued pop sound?

A) 1989
B) Folklore
C) Midnights
D) Evermore

160. Which magazine ranked Taylor Swift 102nd on the list of the 200 Greatest Singers of All Time in 2023?

A) Time
B) Rolling Stone
C) Billboard
D) Vogue

161. Which genre did Taylor Swift embrace in "Folklore" and "Evermore"?

A) Alternative and indie rock
B) Hip hop and trap
C) Country and folk
D) Synth-pop and EDM

162. What did The Los Angeles Times mention as Taylor Swift's defining vocal feature?

A) Intimacy over power
B) Detached cadences
C) Percussion instrument style
D) Nasal and pitch-perfect

163. Which album did Taylor Swift describe as her first "documented, official pop album"?

A) 1989
B) Folklore
C) Lover
D) Red

164. What vocal range does Taylor Swift possess?

A) Soprano
B) Alto
C) Mezzo-soprano
D) Tenor

165. How did critics describe Taylor Swift's vocals in the "Reputation" era?

A) Nasal and pitch-perfect
B) Cool, conversational, and detached
C) Powerful and resonant
D) Weak and strained

166. Which album marked Taylor Swift's shift to alternative, folk, and indie rock styles?

A) Lover
B) Folklore
C) Reputation
D) 1989

167. Which element did critics appreciate in Taylor Swift's live vocals during the Eras Tour?

A) Nasal and pitch-perfect
B) Clarity and tone
C) Cool and detached cadences
D) Percussion instrument style

168. What did Taylor Swift mention as her primary identity in songwriting?

2.A) A dancer
3.B) A singer
4.C) A songwriter
5.D) An actress

169. How does Taylor Swift divide her songwriting into three types?

A) Pencil lyrics, Marker lyrics, Crayon lyrics
B) Quill lyrics, Fountain pen lyrics, Glitter gel pen lyrics
C) Old-fashioned lyrics, Modern lyrics, Lively lyrics
D) Emotional lyrics, Romantic lyrics, Nostalgic lyrics

170. Which award did Taylor Swift receive in 2021, recognizing her as a Songwriter Icon?

A) Grammy Award
B) MTV Music Award
C) National Music Publishers' Association Award
D) Billboard Music Award

171. In 2023, what did Adrian Horton of The Guardian praise about Taylor Swift's performance on the Eras Tour?

A) Her elaborate theatricality
B) Her seemingly endless stamina
C) Her live band collaboration
D) Her intimate solo acoustic performances

172. Which instrument does Taylor Swift often accompany herself with during her performances?
A) Trumpet
B) Banjo
C) Violin
D) Saxophone

173. What was the dominant theme of Taylor Swift's early songs on her first three studio albums?

A) Adventure
B) Love, heartbreak, and insecurities
C) Rebellion
D) Political commentary

174. Which album of Taylor Swift explored the tumult of toxic relationships?

A) Fearless
B) Red
C) 1989
D) Reputation

175. According to The New Yorker, how was Taylor Swift generally portrayed in the media?

A) A Dylanesque visionary
B) A skilled technician
C) A political activist
D) A carefree entertainer

176. Which track of every Swift album is often considered the most emotionally vulnerable?

A) The first track
B) The fifth track
C) The tenth track
D) The last track

177. What did Taylor Swift welcome in her songwriting direction for Folklore and Evermore?

A) Worrying about commercial success
B) Escapism and romanticism
C) Tabloid attention
D) Imposing personal experiences

178. Which two original poems did Taylor Swift publish?

A) "Love Story" and "Eternal Flame"
B) "Blank Space" and "Shake It Off"
C) "Why She Disappeared" and "If You're Anything Like Me"
D) "Bad Blood" and "Style"

179. Which association named Taylor Swift the Songwriter-Artist of the Decade in 2022?

A) Grammy Awards
B) Nashville Songwriters Association International
C) American Music Awards
D) MTV Music Awards

180. What did Taylor Swift explore on her 2020 albums Folklore and Evermore, according to Spin?

A) Pop music
B) Complex emotions with precision and devastation
C) Political themes
D) Commercial success

181. Despite her success, Taylor Swift has faced challenges, including house break-ins and stalkers, some of whom were:

A) Celebrity enthusiasts
B) Armed
C) Paparazzi
D) Innocuous fans

182. Which album detailed Taylor Swift's realization of the "full spectrum of love"?

A) Red
B) 1989
C) Reputation
D) Lover

183. Which album by Taylor Swift embraced nostalgia and post-romance positivity?

A) Fearless
B) Red
C) 1989
D) Lover

184. How did Taylor Swift's "diaristic" technique for songwriting begin?

A) Identifying a melody first
B) Identifying an emotion first, followed by a melody
C) Collaborating with other songwriters
D) Writing lyrics randomly

185. Which publication called Taylor Swift "pop's most approachable superstar"?

A) Rolling Stone
B) Variety
C) The Week
D) NPR

186. What was the inspiration behind Taylor Swift's album Red?

A) Toxic relationships
B) Love and heartbreak
C) Escapism and romanticism
D) The downsides of fame

187. What did Taylor Swift explore on her album 1989?

A) Toxic relationships
B) Escapism and romanticism
C) Nostalgia and post-romance positivity
D) The downsides of fame

188. Which album by Taylor Swift delved into the tumult of toxic relationships?

A) Speak Now
B) Fearless
C) Red
D) 1989

189. What was the inspiration behind Taylor Swift's album Reputation?

A) Toxic relationships
B) Love and heartbreak
C) The downsides of fame
D) Nostalgia and post-romance positivity

190. For which music video did Taylor Swift serve as an executive producer for the interactive app AMEX Unstaged: Taylor Swift Experience?

A) Blank Space
B) Bad Blood
C) Shake It Off
D) You Need to Calm Down

191. Which Taylor Swift production won a Grammy Award for Best Music Video in 2016?

A) Shake It Off
B) Bad Blood
C) Blank Space
D) Style

192. Which album does the music video "Blank Space" belong to?

A) 1989
B) Red
C) Fearless
D) Reputation

193. In 2018, Taylor Swift ventured into sole direction for the music video of which song?

A) Me!
B) You Need to Calm Down
C) Lover
D) The Man

194. Which director did Taylor Swift collaborate with for the music video of "Me!"?

A) Joseph Kahn
B) Roman White
C) Dave Meyers
D) Drew Kirsch

195. For which music video did Taylor Swift win the MTV Video Music Award for Best Direction?

A) The Man
B) Me!
C) You Need to Calm Down
D) Lover

196. What is the name of Taylor Swift's production company credited with producing her visual media starting from the Reputation Stadium Tour?

A) Swift Productions
B) Red Records
C) Taylor Swift Films
D) Taylor Swift Productions

197. For which music video did Taylor Swift co-direct with Roman White?

A) Bad Blood
B) Mine
C) Blank Space
D) Mean

198. What is the name of Taylor Swift's concert documentary in 2018?

A) Speak Now
B) Red Tour
C) Reputation Stadium Tour
D) Fearless Tour

199. Which Taylor Swift music video did she co-direct with Drew Kirsch?

A) Me!
B) You Need to Calm Down
C) Lover
D) The Man

200. What was the first Taylor Swift-directed film?

A) Blank Space
B) All Too Well: The Short Film
C) Bad Blood
D) You Need to Calm Down

201. Which filmmaker has Taylor Swift cited as one of her influences?

A) Quentin Tarantino
B) Chloé Zhao
C) Christopher Nolan
D) Steven Spielberg

202. For which music video did Taylor Swift win the Grammy Award for Best Music Video as a sole director?

A) The Man
B) All Too Well: The Short Film
C) You Need to Calm Down
D) Lover

203. Which Taylor Swift album features the music video "You Need to Calm Down"?

A) 1989
B) Reputation
C) Lover
D) Folklore

204. What is the name of the app associated with the music video "Blank Space"?

A) Swift Experience
B) Unstaged
C) AMEX Unleashed
D) Taylor's World

205. What concept did Taylor Swift develop for the music video "Mean" in 2011?

A) Time Travel
B) School Life
C) Anti-Bullying
D) Love Story

206. For which music video did Taylor Swift collaborate with American Express?

A) Shake It Off
B) Blank Space
C) Bad Blood
D) You Need to Calm Down

207. In which year did Taylor Swift win a Grammy Award for Best Music Video as a sole director?

A) 2020
B) 2021
C) 2022
D) 2023

208. How many Guinness World Records has Taylor Swift won according to the information provided?

A) 50
B) 100
C) 117
D) 150

209. What is the cumulative ticket sales for Taylor Swift's tours, making her the world's highest-grossing female touring act?

A) $1.5 billion
B) $1.8 billion
C) $1.96 billion
D) $2 billion

210. Which magazine included Taylor Swift on its annual list of the 100 most influential people in 2010, 2015, and 2019?

A) Forbes
B) Time
C) Rolling Stone
D) Billboard

211. Taylor Swift was recognized as one of the "Silence Breakers" in 2017 for speaking up about what?

A) Environmental issues
B) Economic inequality
C) Sexual assault
D) Political activism

212. What was Taylor Swift's rank on Forbes' list of the 100 most powerful women in 2023?

A) 10th
B) 5th
C) 20th
D) 1st

213. In Luminate Data history, Taylor Swift holds the record for having how many albums sell over a million copies in a week?

A) Four
B) Five
C) Six
D) Seven

214. Which tour by Taylor Swift is recognized as the highest-grossing tour ever by a woman as of August 2023?

A) Red Tour
B) Fearless Tour
C) 1989 World Tour
D) Eras Tour

215. What did Taylor Swift receive from New York University on May 18, 2022?

A) Grammy Award
B) Doctor of Fine Arts degree
C) MTV Video Music Award
D) Emmy Award

216. How many Grammy Awards has Taylor Swift won, including three for Album of the Year?

A) 8
B) 10
C) 12
D) 15

217. In 2015, Taylor Swift was named the youngest person on Rolling Stone's list of what?

A) Highest-paid musicians
B) 100 Greatest Songwriters of All Time
C) Most influential people
D) Top-selling artists

218. What is the highest income earned by Taylor Swift on Chinese digital music platforms as of 2021?

A) RMB 100,000,000
B) RMB 159,000,000
C) RMB 200,000,000
D) RMB 250,000,000

219. Which country awarded Taylor Swift the Pinnacle Award at the Country Music Association Awards?

A) United States
B) United Kingdom
C) Australia
D) Canada

220. What is the significance of Taylor Swift's appearance on the Billboard Global 200 chart?

A) Most number-one albums
B) Most simultaneous entries
C) Longest-reigning act
D) Most Grammy Awards

221. How many songs did Taylor Swift simultaneously chart on the Billboard Global 200, according to the information provided?

A) 20
B) 25
C) 31
D) 35

222. What is Taylor Swift's rank on the Billboard Artist 100 for the longest-reigning act?

A) 50 weeks
B) 75 weeks
C) 91 weeks
D) 100 weeks

223. How many Brit Awards has Taylor Swift won?

A) One
B) Two
C) Three
D) Four

224. What is the record set by Taylor Swift on Spotify for the most streams in one day?

A) 150 million
B) 200 million
C) 250 million
D) 300 million

225. At the 64th BMI Awards, what award was Taylor Swift the first woman to receive?

A) Grammy Award
B) Emmy Award
C) BMI Award
D) Brit Award

226. What term is used to describe Taylor Swift's fan base?

A) Beliebers
B) Swifties
C) Directioners
D) Arianators

227. In the streaming-dominated industry, Taylor Swift's million-selling albums are considered:

A) Commonplace
B) Anomaly
C) Traditional
D) Unsuccessful

228. During her early career, Taylor Swift was labeled "America's Sweetheart" for her:

A) Bold persona
B) Girl-next-door persona
C) Rebellious attitude
D) Mysterious image

229. What platform did Taylor Swift pioneer as a marketing tool early in her career?

A) Instagram
B) Myspace
C) YouTube
D) Pinterest

230. Which demographic experienced an upsurge in guitar sales, attributed to the "Taylor Swift factor"?

A) Men
B) Teenagers
C) Elderly
D) Women

231. Billboard executive director Jason Lipshutz, Says that Taylor Swift excels in:

A) Live performances
B) Radio presence
C) Streaming
D) All of the above

232. What title did Taylor Swift earn from Billboard for her impact in the 2010s?

A) Woman of the Year
B) Artist of the Year
C) Woman of the Decade
D) Global Icon

233. In what way did Taylor Swift influence industry practices, prompting changes in streaming policies?

A) Reshaping ticketing models
B) Raising awareness of intellectual property
C) Pioneering internet marketing
D) Shaping modern country music

234. Which senior artist considered Taylor Swift the Beatles' successor?

A) Paul McCartney
B) Mick Jagger
C) Madonna
D) Britney Spears

235. What did Carole King call Taylor Swift, acknowledging her contribution to the musical legacy?

A) Professional daughter
B) Torchbearer
C) Icon of the era
D) Millennial Bruce Springsteen

236. Which artist labeled Taylor Swift as "the most iconic pop woman of our generation"?

A) Ariana Grande
B) Billie Eilish
C) Britney Spears
D) Madonna

237. how did Taylor Swift's personal and vulnerable songwriting impact later singers?

A) It discouraged them
B) It made space for them to do the same
C) It influenced their fashion choices
D) It led to fewer album sales

238. Which genre did Taylor Swift help shape in the modern music scene?

A) Pop
B) Hip-hop
C) Country
D) Rock

239. How did Taylor Swift change the music landscape with her discography?

A) By sticking to one genre
B) By ignoring cultural shifts
C) By accommodating cultural shifts
D) By avoiding mainstream music

240. What is Taylor Swift known for in her album rollouts?

A) Cryptic teasers
B) Exclusive interviews
C) Live performances
D) Fashion collaborations

241. In the business realm, Taylor Swift has endorsed which of the following?

A) McDonald's
B) Nike
C) AT&T
D) Coca-Cola

242. Which management team is responsible for Taylor Swift's affairs?

A) 13 Management
B) Swift Enterprises
C) Media Maven
D) Star Power Management

243. Taylor Swift became the global ambassador for which city in 2014?

A) London
B) Paris
C) New York City
D) Tokyo

244. What term do publications use to describe Taylor Swift's discography?

A) Music Galaxy
B) Song Haven
C) Melody Universe
D) Music Universe

245. Taylor Swift released a number of fragrances with which brand?

A) Chanel
B) Elizabeth Arden
C) Gucci
D) Dolce & Gabbana

246. Which National Hockey League team was Taylor Swift a spokesperson for?

A) Chicago Blackhawks
B) Nashville Predators
C) New York Rangers
D) Toronto Maple Leafs

247. What is a common practice in contemporary pop music that became popular because of Taylor Swift?

A) Lip Sync Battles
B) Dance Challenges
C) Cryptic Teasers
D) Virtual Concerts

248. What movement is Taylor Swift a founding signatory of, advocating against sexual harassment?

A) #MeToo movement
B) Time's Up movement
C) March for Our Lives movement
D) Black Lives Matter movement

249. Which organization did Taylor Swift donate to, supporting LGBT rights and equality?

A) ACLU (American Civil Liberties Union)
B) Human Rights Campaign
C) Tennessee Equality Project
D) GLAAD (Gay & Lesbian Alliance Against Defamation)

250. In 2019, where did Taylor Swift perform during WorldPride NYC to show support for gay rights?

A) Central Park
B) The Stonewall Inn
C) Madison Square Garden
D) Times Square

251. What did Taylor Swift urge her fans to do in 2020, resulting in 65,000 people registering to vote within one day?

A) Donate to charity
B) Check their voter registration
C) Attend a protest
D) Boycott a specific brand

252. Which movement and cause is Taylor Swift a vocal critic of, especially following the George Floyd protests?

A) Climate change awareness
B) Animal rights
C) White supremacy, racism, and police brutality
D) Education reform

253. What did Taylor Swift call for in 2020 to become a national holiday, as part of her advocacy for racial justice?

A) Martin Luther King Jr. Day
B) Independence Day
C) Juneteenth
D) Veterans Day

254. During the U.S. presidential election, whom did Taylor Swift endorse?

A) Bernie Sanders
B) Joe Biden and Kamala Harris
C) Donald Trump
D) Elizabeth Warren

255. In which year did Taylor Swift become the highest-paid celebrity, setting a Guinness World Record for the highest annual earnings ever for a female musician?

A) 2015
B) 2016
C) 2017
D) 2018

256. In which album can you find the Taylor Swift song "Should've Said No"?

A) Fearless
B) Speak Now
C) Red
D) 1989

257. Taylor Swift was awarded the Nickelodeon Kids' Choice Awards for her dedication to helping others?

A) Golden Heart Award
B) Big Help Award
C) Star of Compassion
D) Philanthropy Achievement Award

258. Taylor Swift donated during a telethon hosted by WSMV to help the victims of the Tennessee floods?

A) $250,000
B) $500,000
C) $750,000
D) $1 million

259. Which organization did Taylor Swift donate to during the COVID-19 pandemic to support relief efforts?

A) Red Cross
B) Feeding America
C) World Health Organization
D) UNICEF

260. Which charitable organization did Taylor Swift support in honor of Sexual Assault Awareness and Prevention Month in 2021?

A) RAINN
B) American Red Cross
C) Save the Children
D) Doctors Without Borders

261. What is the name of Taylor Swift's ongoing sixth concert tour?

A) Revival Tour
B) Eras Tour
C) Reputation Stadium Tour
D) Midnights Tour

262. In which city did the Eras Tour commence?

A) Los Angeles
B) Glendale
C) Chicago
D) New York

263. How many shows are included in Taylor Swift's Eras Tour?
A) 151
B) 100
C) 50
D) 200

264. Which album did Taylor Swift release the re-recorded version of during the Eras Tour?

A) Fearless
B) Speak Now
C) 1989
D) Reputation

265. What is the total duration of the Eras Tour show?

A) 2 hours
B) 3 hours
C) 4 hours
D) 3.5 hours

266. Which song became a single during the Eras Tour?

A) Cruel Summer
B) Karma
C) I Can See You
D) Blank Space

267. When is the scheduled end date of the Eras Tour?

A) December 8, 2023
B) October 13, 2024
C) March 17, 2024
D) December 8, 2024

268. Which company faced scrutiny for alleged monopoly during the Eras Tour ticket sales?

A) StubHub
B) Ticketmaster
C) Live Nation
D) AXS

269. In which month and year did the Eras Tour start?

A) October 2022
B) March 2023
C) August 2023
D) December 2023

270. How many continents does the Eras Tour cover?

A) 3
B) 4
C) 5
D) 6

271. What impact did the Eras Tour have on businesses and tourism?

A) Decreased tourism
B) No impact on businesses
C) Elevated economies, businesses, and tourism
D) Negative impact on economies

272. Which album does "Cruel Summer" belong to?

A) Red
B) 1989
C) Speak Now
D) Midnights

273. Which month and year was the Eras Tour concert film released?

A) October 2022
B) March 2023
C) August 2023
D) October 2023

274. What is the primary concept of the Eras Tour?

A) Journey through Taylor Swift's fashion evolution
B) Journey through her musical eras
C) A focus on her personal life
D) Exploration of various music genres

275. Which company was scrutinized for ineffective sales during the Eras Tour?

A) StubHub
B) Ticketmaster
C) Live Nation
D) AXS

276. What is the total number of songs in the Eras Tour set list?

A) 44
B) 30
C) 50
D) 60

277. How many acts are there in the Eras Tour, each portraying the albums conceptually?

A) 5
B) 8
C) 10
D) 12

278. Due to the COVID-19 pandemic in 2020, which tour of Taylor Swift got canceled?

A) Fearless Tour
B) Red Tour
C) 1989 World Tour
D) Lover Fest

279. Who is listed as a supporting act for "The Eras Tour" from the given options?

A) Ariana Grande
B) Beabadoobee
C) Ed Sheeran
D) Justin Bieber

280. Which continent is not listed as a location for "The Eras Tour"?

A) Asia
B) Europe
C) Antarctica
D) South America

281. What is the total duration of "The Eras Tour" in months?

A) 18
B) 9
C) 12
D) 7

282. Which talk shows did Taylor Swift appear on in October 2022 to promote her album Midnights?

A) The Ellen DeGeneres Show
B) The Tonight Show Starring Jimmy Fallon
C) The Late Show with Stephen Colbert
D) Jimmy Kimmel Live!

283. How many shows were initially announced for the Eras Tour across 20 US cities?

A) 27
B) 38
C) 52
D) 17

284. Which company, now bankrupt, was in talks for a sponsorship deal with Taylor Swift's Eras Tour?

A) Coinbase
B) FTX
C) Binance
D) Kraken

285. On what date did Taylor Swift announce the second US leg of the Eras Tour in 2024?

A) January 31
B) November 4
C) August 3
D) November 1

286. Who served as the tour's promoter for the Eras Tour?

A) Messina Touring Group
B) Live Nation
C) AEG Presents
D) Ticketmaster

287. How many additional shows were added to some US cities due to popular demand for the Eras Tour?

A) 4
B) 8
C) 12
D) 17

288. What did Billboard describe the Eras Tour announcement as?

A) Calm and composed
B) "the must-see blockbuster of the year"
C) Predictable
D) Ordinary

289. When did Taylor Swift make tour merchandise inspired by all of her ten album "eras" available for purchase?

A) November 1
B) January 31
C) August 3
D) November 4

290. did Taylor Swift announce as the opener for the second US leg of the Eras Tour in 2024?

A) Paramore
B) Haim
C) Gracie Abrams
D) Phoebe Bridgers

291. Which entertainment group partnered with Messina Touring Group to promote the Eras Tour?

A) Live Nation
B) AEG Presents
C) Ticketmaster
D) MGM Resorts

292. On which morning show did Taylor Swift announce the Eras Tour on November 1?

A) Good Morning America
B) Today Show
C) CBS This Morning
D) The Early Show

293. What was the most extensive US tour of Taylor Swift's career before the Eras Tour?

A) Red Tour
B) Reputation Stadium Tour
C) Fearless Tour
D) Lover Fest

294. Which artist did not serve as an opening act for the Eras Tour?

A) Paramore
B) Haim
C) Ed Sheeran
D) Phoebe Bridgers

295. Who was the last opener announced for the Eras Tour on August 3, 2023?

A) Gracie Abrams
B) Paramore
C) Haim
D) Phoebe Bridgers

296. What singer was announced as the opening act for the Latin American shows of Taylor Swift's Eras Tour?

A) Sabrina Carpenter
B) Louta
C) Paramore
D) Abrams

297. On which date did Taylor Swift announce the Latin American shows of the Eras Tour?

A) June 6
B) June 12
C) June 20
D) June 2

298. Which country demanded the Eras Tour to be brought to their city but was absent in the initial announcement?

A) Canada
B) China
C) Mexico
D) Argentina

299. What reason was cited for the lack of shows in Malaysia during the Eras Tour announcement?

A) Infrastructure concerns
B) Legal opposition to LGBT rights
C) COVID-19 pandemic lockdowns
D) Technical malfunctions

300. In the Asia-Pacific, how many additional shows were announced for Singapore during the Eras Tour?

A) Two
B) Four
C) Six
D) Eight

301. Who was announced as the opening act for the European leg of the Eras Tour?

A) Sabrina Carpenter
B) Paramore
C) Abrams
D) Louta

302. Which country experienced delayed reopening after the COVID-19 pandemic, affecting touring plans for the Eras Tour?

A) Japan
B) Singapore
C) Hong Kong
D) Philippines

303. Which artist was announced as the opening act for the London shows during the European leg of the Eras Tour?

A) Paramore
B) Abrams
C) Louta
D) Sabrina Carpenter

304. What was the reason for not including many Asian countries in the Eras Tour?

A) Lack of interest
B) Infrastructure concerns
C) Language barriers
D) Political protests

305. Where does Taylor Swift have real estate properties as part of her impressive portfolio?

A) Phoenix, Arizona
B) Tribeca, Manhattan
C) Boston, Massachusetts
D) Austin, Texas

306. **What is Taylor's favorite number?**

A) 24
B) 15
C) 22
D) 13

307. What is at least one of Taylor Swift's cat's names?

A) Lucifer
B) Bella
C) Olivia
D) Anamaria

308. How did Taylor Swift uniquely make her entrance onto the stage during the Eras Tour?

A) Smuggled inside a janitorial cart
B) Slingshotted from the top of the venue
C) Disguised as a crew member
D) A hoverboard

309. What original song has Taylor Swift performed live the most?

A)"Our Song"
B)"You Belong With Me"
C)"Shake It Off"
D)"Love Story"

310. Which city had an additional show announced due to high demand after the public sale commenced?

A) Rio de Janeiro
B) Mexico City
C) Buenos Aires
D) São Paulo

311. How many extra shows were announced in Australia for the Eras Tour?

A) Four
B) Two
C) Six
D) Eight

312. Who was announced as an additional opening act for the Buenos Aires show during the Eras Tour?

A) Sabrina Carpenter
B) Louta
C) Paramore
D) Abrams

313. What was the primary reason for Taylor Swift's partnership with Capital One in relation to ticket sales for her tour?

A) Brand promotion
B) Enhanced security measures
C) Exclusive presale access
D) Reduced ticket prices

314. How did fans receive boosts for the TaylorSwiftTix Presale access?

A) Purchasing tickets from Ticketmaster
B) Registering for the Royal Bank of Canada's Avion Rewards program
C) Purchasing merchandise from Swift's website
D) Camping outside the venue

315. What price range did Taylor Swift confirm for the tickets in advance, abandoning the "platinum ticket" model?

A) $99 to $599
B) $49 to $449
C) $199 to $899
D) $299 to $799

316. According to Ticketmaster, what was the purpose of the TaylorSwiftTix Presale?

A) Ensure VIP packages are sold
B) Avoid bots and scalpers
C) Increase ticket prices
D) Select fans randomly for presale access

317. Which bank's clients received exclusive access to a separate presale for Canadian ticket sales?

A) Royal Bank of Canada
B) Banco Patagonia
C) Capital One
D) C6 Bank

318. What percentage of Canada's population registered for the Toronto Verified Fan presale?

A) 50%
B) 77%
C) 60%
D) 40%

319. In Mexico, which program handled the ticket presale for Taylor Swift's tour?

A) Banco Patagonia's Verified Fan program
B) Avion Rewards program
C) TaylorSwiftTix Presale
D) Ticketmaster's Verified Fan program

320. What did fans in Brazil do instantly after the announcement of the shows on June 2?

A) Queue for physical tickets
B) Register for the Verified Fan program
C) Purchase tickets online
D) Camp outside the venue

321. For the Brazil shows, which cardholders gained access to presales on June 6 and 10?

A) Capital One
B) Royal Bank of Canada
C) C6 Bank Mastercard
D) Banco Patagonia

322. Which company served as Swift's tour promotion partner in Argentina?

A) Ticketmaster
B) Avion Rewards program
C) DF Entertainment
D) Capital One

323. What was the price range for VIP packages for Taylor Swift's tour?

A) $99 to $599
B) $49 to $449
C) $199 to $899
D) $299 to $799

324. Which Australian state declared the Eras Tour a "major event," penalizing scalping and misleading advertisement?

A) Queensland
B) Victoria
C) New South Wales
D) Western Australia

325. Which cardholders in Southeast Asia had presale access for the Singaporean shows?

A) Visa
B) MasterCard
C) American Express
D) United Overseas Bank (UOB)

326. What company's website crashed due to the high demand for VIP packages on June 26?

A) Ticketmaster
B) Viagogo
C) Ticketek
D) Klook

327. How many bot purchase attempts did Ticketek state it neutralized during the presale?

A) 50 million
B) 100 million
C) 500 million
D) 1 billion

328. How many users were in the virtual queue for UOB cardholders' presale in Southeast Asia?

A) 100,000
B) 500,000
C) 1 million
D) 5 million

329. How many users registered for access to the available tickets during the general sale in Southeast Asia?

A) 5 million
B) 10 million
C) 15 million
D) 22 million

330. Which venue sold tickets coupled with hotel stays and other experiences for the Singaporean shows?

A) Marina Bay Sands
B) Resorts World Sentosa
C) Suntec Singapore Convention & Exhibition Centre
D) Singapore Indoor Stadium

331. Which country's fans purchased travel packages along with tickets for the Singaporean shows?

A) Australia
B) Thailand
C) Indonesia
D) Philippines

332. Which stadium in London experienced unprecedented demand for Taylor Swift's tickets?

A) Wembley Stadium
B) Principality Stadium
C) Old Trafford
D) Emirates Stadium

333. Which company handled the ticket sales for the United Kingdom?

A) AXS
B) Ticketmaster
C) See Tickets
D) Viagogo

334. Which country reported website crashes during the ticket sale but highlighted the illegality of reselling tickets above face value?

A) France
B) Germany
C) United Kingdom
D) Ireland

335. Which company responded to the widespread scalping of the tour's UK tickets?

A) See Tickets
B) StubHub
C) Viagogo
D) Ticketmaster

336. Which concept does the Eras Tour's staging primarily focus on? Options:

A) Time travel
B) Worldbuilding
C) Virtual reality
D) Futuristic technology

337. Who choreographed the 15 backup dancers for the Eras Tour? Options:

A) Taylor Swift
B) Mandy Moore
C) Emma Stone
D) Roberto Cavalli

338. What is the central theme of the Eras Tour's wardrobe? Options:

A) Monochrome colors
B) Vintage fashion
C) Tribute to albums
D) Sci-fi aesthetics

339. How did Taylor Swift physically prepare for the Eras Tour? Options:

A) Yoga and meditation
B) Running on a treadmill
C) Weightlifting
D) Swimming

340. Which designer created the sequined tulle ball gown for the Speak Now act?

A) Atelier Versace
B) Zuhair Murad
C) Roberto Cavalli
D) Oscar de la Renta

341. Which designer was recommended by Emma Stone for the Eras Tour's costumes?

A) Mandy Moore
B) Roberto Cavalli
C) Oscar de la Renta
D) Elie Saab

342. How many hours of atelier handwork were required for the sequined tulle ball gown?

A) 170 hours
B) 250 hours
C) 350 hours
D) 500 hours

343. Which designer designed the Fearless, 1989, and Reputation acts' costumes with Swarovski crystals?

A) Roberto Cavalli
B) Zuhair Murad
C) Ashish
D) Fausto Puglisi

344. How many months did Taylor Swift train in dance leading up to the first Eras Tour show?

A) 1 month
B) 3 months
C) 6 months
D) 12 months

345. What record did the Eras Tour by Taylor Swift break in the first day of the US presale?

A) Most shows performed in a single day
B) Highest attendance in a single concert
C) Most tickets sold by an artist in a single day
D) Longest concert tour in history

346. Which country proposed the "Taylor Swift Law" to penalize scalpers?

A) United States
B) Brazil
C) United Kingdom
D) Australia

347. During the Eras Tour, what did Taylor Swift donate at every stop as reported by respective organizations?

A) Clothing
B) Food bank units
C) Musical instruments
D) Scholarships

348. How much did Taylor Swift reportedly give as bonus payments to her entire touring crew at the conclusion of the first US leg?

A) $5 million
B) $25 million
C) $55 million
D) $100 million

349. What was the reported cause of Ana Clara Benevides' death in Brazil?

A) Cardiac arrest due to heat exhaustion
B) Injuries from a stampede
C) Drug overdose
D) Dehydration

350. Why did Taylor Swift postpone a show in Brazil from November 18 to November 20?

A) Technical issues
B) Extreme temperatures
C) Political interference
D) Artist's health

351. What did Taylor Swift arrange and distribute to the crowd during the Rio de Janeiro show?

A) Merchandise
B) Food
C) Water bottles
D) Concert tickets

352. In which city does Taylor Swift perform at the Hard Rock Stadium in the United States on October 18, 2024?

A) Miami Gardens
B) New Orleans
C) Indianapolis
D) Toronto

353. Who is the dance captain in Taylor Swift's team?

A) Amanda Balen
B) Taylor Banks
C) Audrey Douglass
D) Tori Evans

354. How did the Eras Tour impact Taylor Swift's net worth?

A) It had no effect on her net worth
B) It decreased her net worth
C) It increased her net worth to $1.1 billion
D) It remained constant at $740 million

355. What record did the Eras Tour by Taylor Swift break in the first day of the US presale?

A) Most shows performed in a single day
B) Highest attendance in a single concert
C) Most tickets sold by an artist in a single day
D) Longest concert tour in history

356. What was the primary reason for Taylor Swift taking a break from touring before announcing the Eras Tour?

A) Personal reasons
B) Impact of the COVID-19 pandemic
C) Creative hiatus
D) Contractual obligations

357. Which world leader wrote to Taylor Swift, requesting her to bring the Eras Tour to Chile?

A) Justin Trudeau
B) Gabriel Boric
C) Gergely Karácsony
D) Grant Robertson

358. What impact did the Eras Tour have on Canada initially, leading to government displeasure?

A) Increased tourism
B) Economic boost
C) Canada was initially snubbed
D) Enhanced diplomatic relations

359. In which countries did the Eras Tour face political demands and expressions of dismay?

A) Canada and Australia
B) Chile and Hungary
C) Thailand and Taiwan
D) All of the above

360. Which Australian cities expressed dismay at the Eras Tour not visiting them?

A) Sydney and Melbourne
B) Brisbane and Adelaide
C) Perth and Sydney
D) Melbourne and Brisbane

361. Why did New Zealand finance minister Grant Robertson express disappointment despite the tour's popularity?

A) Concerns about crowd control
B) Swift's unpopularity in New Zealand
C) Economic constraints
D) Displeasure with the tour skipping New Zealand

362. Who petitioned Taylor Swift to bring the Eras Tour to Thailand, citing the country's democratic progress?

A) Pita Limjaroenrat
B) Jaw Shaw-kong
C) Gergely Karácsony
D) Grant Robertson

363. In which country did Jaw Shaw-kong claim Taylor Swift declined to perform due to "geopolitical risks"?

A) Japan
B) South Korea
C) Taiwan
D) China

364. What term did financial analysts use to describe the Eras Tour's impact on the economy after the COVID-19 recession?

A) Swift Surge
B) Taylor Economics
C) TSwift Lift
D) Concert Boost

365. How did the Eras Tour impact local businesses?

A) No impact
B) Decreased revenue
C) Not mentioned
D) Boosted local economies

366. What did the Federal Reserve credit Taylor Swift with in relation to the US economy?

A) Economic decline
B) Boosting the economy at large
C) Swift Surge
D) Economic downturn

367. In urban areas, which industry did the Eras Tour particularly boost?

A) Technology
B) Hospitality
C) Manufacturing
D) Agriculture

368. What term did The Wall Street Journal coin to explain the economics involved in and around the Eras Tour?

A) Concertonomics
B) Swift Surge
C) Taylornomics
D) Economic Renaissance

369. How did the Las Vegas Convention and Visitors Authority credit the Eras Tour?

A) Boosting tourism
B) Restoring the economy to pre-pandemic levels
C) Decreasing hotel revenue
D) No impact on the economy

370. What economic impact did the three-day stop in Tampa have, according to reports?

A) Decreased hotel demand
B) Increased taxes for the city
C) No economic impact
D) Swift-themed protests

371. How much hotel revenue did Nashville, Tennessee report from two nights of the Eras Tour?
A) $10 million
B) $28 million
C) No impact on hotel revenue
D) Economic downturn

372. What happened to hotel rooms, restaurant reservations, and train tickets in Boston days before the Eras Tour shows in nearby Foxborough, Massachusetts?

A) Increased availability
B) Swift-themed discounts
C) Sold out
D) No impact on bookings

373. What did Chicago's Eras Tour dates mark in terms of hotel occupancy?

A) No impact
B) Lowest hotel occupancy
C) Highest hotel occupancy in the city's history
D) Economic decline

374. What was the estimated consumer spending in Cincinnati related to the Eras Tour?

A) $10 million
B) $48 million
C) No impact on consumer spending
D) Economic downturn

375. How much revenue did Swift's shows in Mexico City generate, according to reports?

A) $10 million
B) $50 million
C) US$59 million
D) No economic impact

376. Why did airlines, including LATAM, allow fans to rebook flight tickets at no cost?

A) Swift's personal request
B) Bad weather
C) Technical issues
 D) No reason mentioned

377. Who coined the term "Swiftonomics" to describe the economics of the Eras Tour?

A) Taylor Swift
B) Augusta Saraiva
C) Jerome Powell
D) Marina Bay Sands

378. The Eras Tour's six-day residency in which city is part of the government's plan to promote it as Asia's music capital?

A) Los Angeles
B) Singapore
C) Buenos Aires
D) Sydney

379. How much did fans reportedly spend on average per concert for the Eras Tour, according to Business magazine Fortune?

A) $100
B) $500
C) $1,300
D) $2,000

380. Why do some fans experience "post-concert amnesia" according to psychologists?

A) Lack of interest in the concert
B) Overwhelming happy emotions
C) Traumatic events during the show
D) Excessive information provided

381. How did fans outside the Eras Tour venues contribute to the phenomenon known as "Taylor-gating"?

A) They organized protests
B) They performed flash mobs
C) They gathered for tailgate parties
D) They boycotted the concerts

382. In what city's shows of the Eras Tour around 20,000 ticketless fans gathered every night?

A) Nashville
B) Tampa
C) Chicago
D) Philadelphia

383. Which city were the fans with general admission tickets camping outside the concert venue in tents for five months?

A) Mexico City
B) Buenos Aires
C) Inglewood
D) Kansas City

384. What did fans trade with each other or give to celebrity attendees during the Eras Tour?

A) Stickers
B) Concert tickets
C) Friendship bracelets
D) T-shirts

385. What did Lupita Nyong'o, a celebrity attendee, make and share at the Eras Tour?

A) Posters
B) Hats
C) Friendship bracelets
D) Scarves

386. What specific items experienced increased demand due to Taylor Swift's Eras Tour?

A) Denim jackets
B) Metallic boots
C) Leather gloves
D) Wool scarves

387. How did Swifties at the Eras Tour influence the direction of 2023 summer fashion?

A) They had no influence
B) They influenced winter fashion
C) They shaped the direction of summer fashion
D) They inspired a return to vintage fashion

388. What caused seismic activity during Taylor Swift's tour stop in Seattle on July 22 and 23, 2023?

A) Earthquake
B) Fans' jumping, dancing, and cheering
C) Loud sound system
D) Both B and C

389. What was the magnitude of the seismic activity during Taylor Swift's Seattle concerts, known as the "Swift Quake"?

A) 2.0
B) 2.3
C) 1.5
D) 3.0

390. What did Arlington, Texas do to honor Taylor Swift during the Eras Tour?

A) Ignored the tour
B) Renamed a street to Taylor Swift Way
C) Decreased city attractions
D) Moved the tour venue

391. How did Rio de Janeiro welcome the Eras Tour to Brazil?

A) No welcome
B) Lit the city with fireworks
C) Renamed streets
D) Projected on the statue of Christ the Redeemer

392. How did the Buenos Aires City Legislature honor Taylor Swift?

A) Designated Swift as "Guest of Honor"
B) Declared a city holiday
C) Renamed streets
D) No honor

393. What resolution did the Pennsylvania General Assembly pass in December 2023?

A) No resolution
B) Lit the city with fireworks
C) Renamed streets
D) Recognized 2023 as "the Taylor Swift era" in Pennsylvania

394. What did Starbucks stores across the US do to celebrate the completion of the first US leg of the Eras Tour?

A) Introduced a new Taylor Swift-themed drink
B) Played Taylor Swift's music all day
C) Organized Swift-themed events in stores
D) Offered discounts on Taylor Swift's albums

395. Which skyscraper building displayed a large "Welcome to A-TAY-L" sign for Taylor Swift?

A) Empire State Building
B) Willis Tower
C) Burj Khalifa
D) CN Tower

396. What did Downtown Kansas City do in reference to Speak Now?

A) No reference
B) Lit the city blue
C) Lit the city purple
D) Renamed streets

397. What did Taylorsville, Georgia declare during the Eras Tour?

A) No declaration
B) Declared Taylor Swift Day
C) Renamed the city
D) Ignored the tour

398. What change did Houston make during the Eras Tour?

A) celebrated "The Eras Tour weekend"
B) Renamed the city
C) Lit city hall yellow
D) Distributed sweets

399. The Country Music Hall of Fame and Museum opened an exhibit titled:

A) Taylor Swift's Greatest Hits
B) Through Taylor Swift's Eras
C) Swift's Musical Journey
D) The Evolution of Taylor Swift

400. What did The Wall Street Journal estimate the worth of merchandise sold at every stop of the tour?

A) $1 million
B) $2 million
C) $3 million
D) $4 million

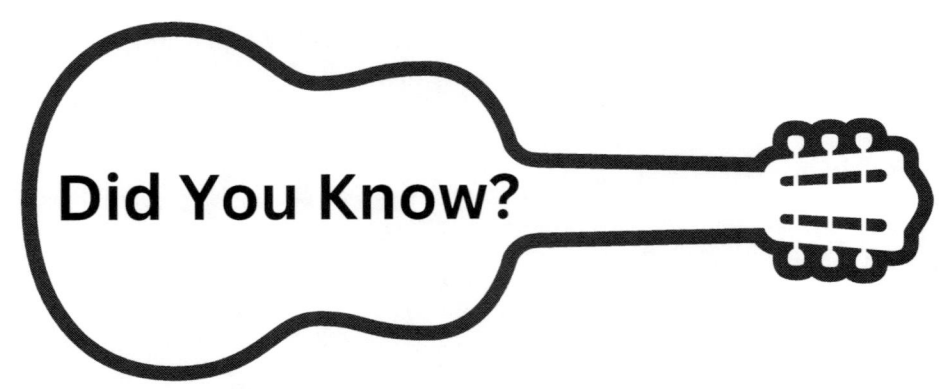

Did You Know?

Did you know Taylor Swift's early years were spent on a Christmas tree farm owned by her father in Pennsylvania?

Did you know Taylor's parents are Scott Kingsley Swift, a former stockbroker, and Andrea Gardner Swift, a former homemaker and mutual fund marketing executive?

Did you know Taylor has a younger brother, Austin Swift, who is an actor?

Did you know Taylor's maternal grandmother, Marjorie Finlay, was an opera singer?

Did you know Taylor attended Alvernia Montessori School and later transferred to the Wyndcroft School?

Did you know that at the age of nine, Taylor Swift became interested in musical theater, performing in several Berks Youth Theatre Academy productions?

Did you know Taylor shifted her focus to country music after being inspired by Shania Twain's songs?

Did you know that at 14, Taylor and her family moved to Hendersonville, Tennessee, to pursue her music career?

Did you know Taylor Swift has been hailed as one of the greatest songwriters ever by various publications?

Did you know Swift identifies herself as a songwriter first, stating, "I write songs, and my voice is just a way to get those lyrics across"?

Did you know her early songs drew inspiration from personal experiences, using a "diaristic" technique of identifying emotions followed by melody?

Did you know Swift's first three albums focused on themes of love, heartbreak, and insecurities from an adolescent perspective?

Did you know her album "Red" delved into the tumult of toxic relationships, while "1989" embraced nostalgia and post-romance positivity?

Did you know "Reputation" was inspired by the downsides of Swift's fame, while "Lover" detailed her realization of the "full spectrum of love"?

Did you know other themes in Swift's music include family dynamics, friendship, alienation, self-awareness, and addressing vitriol, especially sexism?

Did you know on her 2020 albums, "Folklore" and "Evermore," Swift explored fictional narratives, liberating herself from tabloid attention and showcasing new artistic paths?

Did you know Swift co-directed the music video for "Mine" and developed the concept and treatment for "Mean" in 2011?

Did you know Swift's involvement in the crafting of music videos earned her recognition, including a Primetime Emmy Award for Outstanding Interactive Program in 2015?

Did you know she holds 40 American Music Awards, the most won by any artist?

Did you know Swift's production company, Taylor Swift Productions, is credited with producing all her visual media starting with the 2018 concert documentary "Reputation Stadium Tour"?

Did you know after "Folklore: The Long Pond Studio Sessions," Swift debuted as a filmmaker with "All Too Well: The Short Film"? this made her the first artist to win the Grammy Award for Best Music Video as a sole director?

Did you know Taylor Swift has won 12 Grammy Awards, including three for Album of the Year, tying for the most by an artist?

Did you know she is the highest-grossing female touring act ever, with cumulative ticket sales at $1.96 billion as of November 2023?

Did you know "The Eras Tour" is the highest-grossing tour of all time as of December 2023, surpassing $1 billion in revenue?

Did you know Swift is the most streamed female act on Spotify and Apple Music, holding records for daily and monthly streams?

Did you know Taylor Swift is the only artist in Luminate history to have six albums sell over a million copies in a week?

Did you know she was named by Forbes as the fifth-most powerful woman in the world in 2023, the first entertainer ever to place in the top five?

Did you know she has designed American Greetings cards and Jakks Pacific dolls, showcasing her creative involvement in diverse product lines?

Did you know her in-house management team is called 13 Management, a nod to her favorite number?

Did you know Before the release of 1989, Swift invited 89 of her biggest fans over to her house to listen to her album, Taylor also baked cookies for her guests.?

Did you know when Taylor was a kid, she really love Britney Spears. She wrote a song about her titled "Britney and I", but she said she won't publish it?

Did you know Swift has been a spokesperson for the National Hockey League's Nashville Predators and Sony Cyber-shot digital cameras?

Did you know Taylor Swift's net worth is estimated at $1.1 billion as of October 2023, making her the first musician to achieve billionaire status solely through her songs and performances?

Did you know Swift was named the highest-earning female musician by Forbes four times (2016, 2019, 2021, and 2022)?

Did you know Taylor Swift's real estate portfolio is valued at $150 million as of 2023, featuring properties in Nashville, Tribeca, Manhattan, Los Angeles (Samuel Goldwyn Estate), and Rhode Island (High Watch)?

Did you know Swift donated $55 million in bonus payments to her entire crew during the Eras Tour in 2023 and actively supported local businesses?

Did you know she donated $100,000 to the Red Cross for the victims of the Iowa flood in 2008?

Did you know Swift helped shape the modern country music scene, extended her success globally, and pioneered the use of the internet (Myspace) as a marketing tool?

Did you know Swift's ability to be personal and vulnerable in her songs has been credited with making space for later singers like Billie Eilish, Ariana Grande, and Halsey to do the same?

Did you know Kim Kardashian said that "Last Kiss" by Taylor Swift is her favorite song from Taylor?

Do you know that Taylor Swift's concerts in Seattle triggered a seismic event known as the "Swift Quake," reaching a magnitude of 2.3, surpassing the intensity of the famous Beast Quake during an NFL game

Did you know At age 10, Swift was singing at a variety of local events, including contests & fairs.?

Did you know At age 10, Swift was singing at a variety of local events, including contests & fairs.?

Did you know Swift is obsessed with "Disney everything." She even appeared in the Disney feature movie Hannah Montana.?

Do you know that Taylor Swift also owns a Dassault Falcon 900 private jet – and an airport hangar at Nashville International Airport!?

Do you know that Taylor Swift also owns a Dassault Falcon 900 private jet – and an airport hangar at Nashville International Airport!?

Did you know that as of January 8, 2024, Taylor Swift: The Eras Tour has achieved an unprecedented global success, grossing a staggering $261.6 million worldwide, making it the highest-grossing concert or performance film ever?

Were you aware that the film not only debuted at number one but also maintained its position for two consecutive weeks at the U.S. box office, a rare accomplishment for a concert film?

Swift has three cats, With her three kitties, Benjamin Button, Olivia Benson, and Meredith Grey, the pop singer is quite the package. The three cat celebrities frequently feature in advertisements, music videos, public events, and social media posts.

Do you know that She's written a 350-page novel

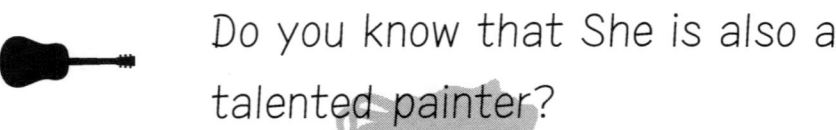

Do you know that She is also a talented painter?

Do you know Her favorite nail polish is BLUE?

Do you know Her favorite dessert is cheesecake?

Do you know Her She wrote "Fearless" on her tour bus?

Do you know Taylor Lautner is her best ex ?

Do you know She is close friends with Selena Gomez ?

Do you know Her song "Haunted" was inspired by Twilight movie ?

Do you know Taylor likes to read up on unusual medical problems ?

Do you know Her favorite ice-cream flavor is chocolate caramel ?

Do you know To Kill A Mockingbird is one of her favorite books ?

Do you know She voice acted the character of Audrey in The Lorax ?

Do you know She calls her car "Toyoat" because it brand is Toyota ?

Do you know She was in the film Valentine's Day in 2010 as Felicia?

Do you know Taylor and Abigail has been a best friend since Taylor was 15 ?

Do you know Her first date was dinner in Nashville and coffe at Starbucks ?

Do you know Taylor Swift is a cat lover and her friends usually call her "cat lady" ?

Do you know that twitter user name taylorswift13 has exactly 13 characters ?

Do you know that "Back To December" is her first apologizing song (for Taylor Lautner) ?

Do you know Taylor also played Rosemary in the film adaptation of The Giver in 2014 ?

Do you know her favorite designers are Marchesa, Badgley Mischka, and Oscar de la Renta ?

Do you know She obsessed with high heels, but rarely wears them out of fear she'll fall ?

Do you know Swift owns an eight-bedroom summer house in coastal Watch Hill, Rhode Island. ?

Do you know One of her favorite items of clothing she likes to wear is a pair of cowboy boots ?

Do you know She won her first BRIT Award for International Female Solo Artist in February 2015. ?

TAYLOR SWIFT QUOTES

"I'm the type of person, I have to study to get an A on the test."

. "I'd like to think you don't stop being creative once you get happy. My ultimate goal is to end up being happy. Most of the time."

"I think songwriting is the ultimate form of being able to make anything that happens in your life productive."

"Even if you're happy with the life you've chosen, you're still curious about the other options."

"My parents taught me never to judge others based on whom they love, what color their skin is, or their religion."

"Nashville is my home, and the reason why I get to do what I love."

"When you're singing you can hear the echo of people in the audience singing every single word with you, and that was that big dream that I had for myself. It's happening."

"Factoring in millions of people when I'm writing a song is not a good idea. I don't ever do it."

"When I get on a roll with something, it's really hard for me to put it down unfinished."

"If I'm gonna write songs about my exes, they can write songs about me. That's how it works."

"It's pretty intense writing about my own life, my own struggles."

"I think that you can love people without it being the great love."

"You can be obsessed with the bad things people say and the good things; either way, you're obsessed with yourself, and I'm not—you can become unhinged so easily."

"Anything you put your mind to and add your imagination into can make your life a lot better and a lot more fun."

"I think, as far as branching out with acting, it would take something really right on the mark to distract me from music, because music is everything to me."

"Part of me feels you can't say you were truly in love if it didn't last. If I end up getting married and having kids, that's when I'll know it's real— because it lasted."

"When I'm 40 and nobody wants to see me in a sparkly dress anymore, I'll be like: 'Cool, I'll just go in the studio and write songs for kids.'"

"Every single one of us has a few months here or there that feel like dark months."

"I have this fear of falling in front of large groups of people. That's why I tend not to wear heels."

"I base a lot of decisions on my gut, and going with an independent label was a good one."

"No matter what happens in life, be good to people. Being good to people is a wonderful legacy to leave behind."

"I'm a songwriter. Everything affects me."

"As your career grows, the list of things that makes you happy should not become smaller, it should become bigger."

"I try to read as much as I can. I try to read an informative article every day. I try to stay read up on our world issues."

"My audience has really become a very diverse group of people. It's not just 15-year-old girls. That's kind of what allows me to write from all the different places I want to write from."

"When we're falling in love or out of it, that's when we most need a song that says how we feel. Yeah, I write a lot of songs about boys. And I'm very happy to do that."

QUIZ ANSWERS

1 B) December 13, 1989
2 B) Taylor Alison Swift
3 B) West Reading, Pennsylvania
4 A) Austin Swift
5 A) Stockbroker
6 C) Marketing Executive
7 B) Wyomissing
8 A) 9
9 A) Shania Twain
10 B) Ronnie Cremer
11 C) 14
12 A) Lucky You
13 B) Dan Dymtrow
14 B) Abercrombie & Fitch
15 A) 13
16 C) Hendersonville High School
17 B) 12
18 B) Faith Hill
19 C) New York City
20 D) Wyomissing Tree Farm
21 C) Marjorie Finlay
22 B) Alvernia Montessori School
23 C) Nashville
24 B) Republic Records
25 C) Red
26 B) 1989
27 D) Music
28 A) Miss Americana
29 B) Taylor Swift
30 A) Scott Borchetta

31 C) 2006
32 A) Teardrops on My Guitar
33 C) 3% stake
34 B) Nathan Chapman
35 B) Songwriter/Artist of the Year
36 B) Our Song
37 D) Taylor Swift
38 B) Joe Jonas
39 C) $120,000
40 A) November 11, 2008
41 C) You Belong with Me
42 A) $63 million
43 A) Best Female Video
44 A) Best Country Song
45 C) Kanye West
46 A) Journey to Fearless
47 B) Best Days of Your Life
48 B) 2009
49 C) Today Was a Fairytale
50 B) Entertainer of the Year
51 B) Taylor Lautner
52 D) Valentine's Day
53 B) Keith Urban
54 B) Kanye West interrupting Swift's acceptance speech
55 C) 5
56 C) Taylor Swift
57 A) You'll Always Find Your Way Back Home and Crazier
58 B) Taylor Lautner
59 A) John Mayer
60 B) Mine

61 C) Mean
62 A) 2010
63 A) We Are Never Ever Getting Back Together
64 B) I Knew You Were Trouble
65 C) Harry Styles
66 A) The Lorax
67 B) 2013
68 B) Speak Now
69 A) Speak Now
70 D) Mean
71 B) Safe & Sound
72 B) 2012
73 C) Red
74 A) Safe & Sound
75 A) Tim McGraw
76 A) The Giver
77 C) Sweeter than Fiction
78 B) Pinnacle Award
79 A) Best Female Albums of All Time
80 C) New Girl
81 D) 1989
82 C) New York City
83 B) Calvin Harris
84 C) 1989 World Tour
85 A) Spotify
86 B) David Mueller
87 B) This Is What You Came For
88 A) Look What You Made Me Do
89 B) 2015
90 A) Lack of artist royalties

91 A) Joe Alwyn
92 B) Better Man
93 B) Nils Sjöberg
94 C) 1989
95 C) 1989
96 B) Zayn Malik
97 C) Look What You Made Me Do
98 B) $345.7 million
99 B) American Music Awards
100 D) Reputation
101 B) November 2017
102 C) Grammy Museum exhibit
103 C) 300,000
104 D) International Female Solo Artist
105 D) Sugarland
106 D) Reputation
107 C) Dick Clark Award for Excellence
108 C) I Don't Wanna Live Forever
109 A) Reputation
110 B) Universal Music Group
111 C) Taylor Swift
112 D) Cruel Summer
113 B) Cats
114 A) Scooter Braun
115 B) Me!
116 A) Me!
117 C) Global Publishing Deal with Universal Music Publishing
118 C) Folklore and Evermore
119 B) Lover
120 C) Bombalurina

121 A) A U.S. number-one album and a number-one song
122 A) Cardigan
123 C) Joe Alwyn
124 B) The Guardian
125 B) Folklore
126 C) Three
127 B) No Body, No Crime
128 C) Video for Good
129 B) Indie Folk and Alternative Rock
130 C) Lover
131 C) You Need to Calm Down
132 B) Jack Antonoff and Aaron Dessner
133 A) First woman to win three times
134 B) Lover
135 A) Miss Americana
136 A) Highest-paid musician in the world
137 D) Lover
138 B) Fearless (Taylor's Version)
139 D) All Too Well (10 Minute Version)
140 C) Electropop
141 A) Grammy Award for Best Music Video
142 B) Speak Now (Taylor's Version)
143 B) Anti-Hero
144 D) Eras Tour
145 A) Spotify
146 C) $1 billion
147 C) Big Red Machine
148 A) Where the Crawdads Sing
149 C) Amsterdam
150 C) 1989 (Taylor's Version)

151 B) Travis Kelce
152 B) Storytelling
153 B) Shania Twain
154 A) Joni Mitchell
155 D) Annie Lennox
156 B) Mezzo-soprano
157 B) "My first documented, official pop album.
158 D) 1989
159 C) Midnights
160 B) Rolling Stone
161 A) Alternative and indie rock
162 C) Percussion instrument style
163 B) Folklore
164 C) Mezzo-soprano
165 B) Cool, conversational, and detached
166 B) Folklore
167 B) Clarity and tone
168 C) Songwriter
169 B) Quill lyrics, Fountain pen lyrics, Glitter gel pen lyrics
170 C) National Music Publishers' Association Award
171 B) Her seemingly endless stamina
172 B) Banjo
173 B) Love, heartbreak, and insecurities
174 D) Reputation
175 B) A skilled technician
176 B) The fifth track
177 B) Escapism and romanticism
178 C) "Why She Disappeared" and "If You're Anything Like Me"
179 B) Nashville Songwriters Association International
180 B) Complex emotions with precision and devastation

181 B) Armed
182 D) Lover
183 D) Lover
184 B) Identifying an emotion first, followed by a melody
185 B) Variety
186 B) Love and heartbreak
187 C) Nostalgia and post-romance positivity
188 C) Red
189 C) The downsides of fame
190 B) Bad Blood
191 B) Bad Blood
192 A) 1989
193 D) The Man
194 C) Dave Meyers
195 A) The Man
196 D) Taylor Swift Productions
197 B) Mine
198 C) Reputation Stadium Tour
199 C) Lover
200 B) All Too Well: The Short Film
201 B) Chloé Zhao
202 B) All Too Well: The Short Film
203 D) Lover
204 C) AMEX Unleashed
205 C) Anti-Bullying
206 C) Bad Blood
207 D) 2023
208 C) 117
209 C) $1.96 billion
210 B) Time

211 C) Sexual assault
212 B) 5th
213 C) Six
214 D) Eras Tour
215 B) Doctor of Fine Arts degree
216 C) 12
217 B) 100 Greatest Songwriters of All Time
218 B) RMB 159,000,000
219 A) United States
220 B) Most simultaneous entries
221 C) 31
222 C) 91 weeks
223 B) Two
224 C) 250 million
225 C) BMI Award
226 B) Swifties
227 B) Anomaly
228 B) Girl-next-door persona
229 B) Myspace
230 D) Women
231 D) All of the above
232 C) Woman of the Decade
233 B) Raising awareness of intellectual property
234 A) Paul McCartney
235 B) Torchbearer
236 C) Britney Spears
237 B) It made space for them to do the same
238 C) Country
239 C) By accommodating cultural shifts
240 A) Cryptic teasers

241 C) AT&T
242 A) 13 Management
243 C) New York City
244 D) Music Universe
245 B) Elizabeth Arden
246 B) Nashville Predators
247 C) Cryptic Teasers
248 B) Time's Up movement
249 C) Tennessee Equality Project
250 B) The Stonewall Inn
251 B) Check their voter registration
252 C) White supremacy, racism, and police brutality
253 C) Juneteenth
254 B) Joe Biden and Kamala Harris
255 B) 2016
256 A) Fearless
257 C) Star of Compassion
258 B) $500,000
259 B) Feeding America
260 B) RAINN
261 B) Eras Tour
262 B) Glendale
263 A) 151
264 C) 1989
265 D) 3.5 hours
266 A) Cruel Summer
267 D) December 8, 2024
268 B) Ticketmaster
269 B) March 2023
270 C) 5

271 C) Elevated economies, businesses, and tourism
272 B) 1989
273 D) October 2023
274 B) Journey through her musical eras
275 B) Ticketmaster
276 A) 44
277 C) 10
278 D) Lover Fest
279 B) Beabadoobee
280 C) Antarctica
281 A) 18
282 B) The Tonight Show Starring Jimmy Fallon
283 A) 27
284 B) FTX
285 C) August 3
286 A) Messina Touring Group
287 B) 8
288 B) the must-see blockbuster of the year
289 B) January 31
290 C) Gracie Abrams
291 B) AEG Presents
292 A) Good Morning America
293 B) Reputation Stadium Tour
294 C) Ed Sheeran
295 A) Gracie Abrams
296 A) Sabrina Carpenter
297 D) June 2
298 A) Canada
299 B) Legal opposition to LGBT rights
300 C) Six

301 B) Paramore
302 C) Hong Kong
303 A) Paramore
304 B) Infrastructure concerns
305 B) Tribeca, Manhattan
306 D) 13
307 C) Olivia
308 A) Smuggled inside a janitorial cart
309 D) "Love Story"
310 C) Buenos Aires
311 B) Two
312 B) Louta
313 C) Exclusive presale access
314 C) Purchasing merchandise from Swift's website
315 B) $49 to $449
316 B) Avoid bots and scalpers
317 A) Royal Bank of Canada
318 B) 77%
319 D) Ticketmaster's Verified Fan program
320 A) Queue for physical tickets
321 C) C6 Bank Mastercard
322 C) DF Entertainment
323 C) $199 to $899
324 B) Victoria
325 D) United Overseas Bank (UOB)
326 C) Ticketek
327 C) 500 million
328 C) 1 million
329 D) 22 million
330 A) Marina Bay Sands

331 D) Philippines
332 A) Wembley Stadium
333 B) Ticketmaster
334 B) France
335 C) Viagogo
336 B) Worldbuilding
337 B) Mandy Moore
338 C) Tribute to albums
339 B) Running on a treadmill
340 B) Zuhair Murad
341 A) Mandy Moore
342 C) 350 hours
343 D) Fausto Puglisi
344 B) 3 months
345 C) Most tickets sold by an artist in a single day
346 B) Brazil
347 B) Food bank units
348 C) $55 million
349 A) Cardiac arrest due to heat exhaustion
350 B) Extreme temperatures
351 C) Water bottles
352 C) Miami Gardens
353 A) Amanda Balen
354 C) It increased her net worth to $1.1 billion
355 C) Most tickets sold by an artist in a single day
356 B) Impact of the COVID-19 pandemic
357 B) Gabriel Boric
358 C) Canada was initially snubbed
359 D) All of the above
360 B) Brisbane and Adelaide

361 D) Displeasure with the tour skipping New Zealand
362 A) Pita Limjaroenrat
363 C) Taiwan
364 C) TSwift Lift
365 D) Boosted local economies
366 B) Boosting the economy at large
367 B) Hospitality
368 C) Taylornomics
369 B) Restoring the economy to pre-pandemic levels
370 B) Increased taxes for the city
371 B) $28 million
372 C) Sold out
373 C) Highest hotel occupancy in the city's history
374 B) $48 million
375 C) US$59 million
376 B) Bad weather
377 B) Augusta Saraiva
378 B) Singapore
379 C) $1,300
380 B) Overwhelming happy emotions
381 C) They gathered for tailgate parties
382 D) Philadelphia
383 B) Buenos Aires
384 C) Friendship bracelets
385 C) Friendship bracelets
386 B) Metallic boots
387 C) They shaped the direction of summer fashion
388 D) Both B and C
389 B) 2.3
390 B) Renamed a street to Taylor Swift Way

391 D) Projected on the statue of Christ the Redeemer
392 A) Designated Swift as "Guest of Honor"
393 D) Recognized 2023 as "the Taylor Swift era" in Pennsylvania
394 B) Played Taylor Swift's music all day
395 B) Willis Tower
396 C) Lit the city purple
397 B) Declared Taylor Swift Day
398 A) celebrated "The Eras Tour weekend"
399 B) Through Taylor Swift's Eras
400 C) $3 million

NOTES

Manufactured by Amazon.ca
Bolton, ON

38151541R00081